How Do I Get a Job?

Leanne Currie-McGhee

ReferencePoint
Press®

San Diego, CA

About the Author

Leanne K. Currie-McGhee has authored over thirty educational books and learns more with each book she writes. She, her husband, Keith, and children, Grace and Sol, reside in Norfolk, Virginia.

© 2024 ReferencePoint Press, Inc.
Printed in the United States

For more information, contact:
ReferencePoint Press, Inc.
PO Box 27779
San Diego, CA 92198
www.ReferencePointPress.com

Picture Credits:
Cover: Shutterstock.com
  6: Stock Photos|Amusement Park/iStock
10: coxy58/Shutterstock
12: Mangostar/Shutterstock
14: Sundry Photography/Shutterstock
18: Kaspars Grinvalds/Shutterstock
21: Uladzik Kryhin/Shutterstock
22: VH-studio/Shutterstock
27: fizkes/Shutterstock
30: JuliusKielaitis/Shutterstock

32: Stock Photos|Help Wanted Sign/iStock
35: Dean Drobot/Shutterstock
37: fizkes/Shutterstock
40: Ground Picture/Shutterstock
43: Ground Picture/Shutterstock
45: fizkes/Shutterstock
47: fizkes/Shutterstock
50: G-Stock Studio/Shutterstock
53: Apex MediaWire/Alamy Stock Photo
55: Ground Picture/Shutterstock

LIBRARY OF CONGRESS CATALOGING-IN-PUBLICATION DATA

Names: Currie-McGhee, L. K. (Leanne K.), author.
Title: How do I get a job? / by Leanne Currie-McGhee.
Description: San Diego, CA : ReferencePoint Press, Inc., [2024] | Series:
   Guide to financial responsibility | Includes bibliographical references
   and index.
Identifiers: LCCN 2022055594 (print) | LCCN 2022055595 (ebook) | ISBN
   9781678205546 (library binding) | ISBN 9781678205553 (ebook)
Subjects: LCSH: Vocational guidance--Juvenile literature. |
   Occupations--Juvenile literature. | Job hunting--Juvenile literature.
Classification: LCC HF5381.2 .C874 2024 (print) | LCC HF5381.2 (ebook) |
   DDC 331.702--dc23/eng/20221116
LC record available at https://lccn.loc.gov/2022055594
LC ebook record available at https://lccn.loc.gov/2022055595

CONTENTS

Changing Market

During the summer of 2022, Emma Stacey, age nineteen, managed a crew that operated the Exterminator, a roller coaster at Kennywood, an amusement park outside of Pittsburgh. During the ride, passengers are strapped inside a giant spinning rat that has to dodge robotic exterminators. Stacey ensured that the crew operated the ride and followed procedures to keep the passengers safe. This was Stacey's fourth summer working at Kennywood—but this time there was one major difference. She was made a manager, which meant an increase in pay from $9.25 an hour in 2021 to $14.25 an hour in 2022.

Like other teens and young adults, Stacey benefited from changes in the job market once businesses reopened after months of shutdowns resulting from the COVID-19 pandemic. Many companies experienced labor shortages. This was due to people either choosing not to come back to work or finding other jobs. As a result, companies began turning to teens and young adults to fill many jobs and were willing to pay higher wages for that work.

Courting Teens and Young Adults

Brisk hiring of younger workers has increased their numbers in the workplace. According to the Bureau of Labor Statistics, in July 2022 the workforce included 20.9 million workers ages sixteen to twenty-four. This number represents an increase over the previous year. In July 2022, 55.3

percent of teens and young adults were employed, which was up from 54.4 percent in July 2021.

Many younger workers have been given opportunities to work at jobs that come with more responsibility and higher pay than they might have enjoyed a few years ago. "In an extremely tight labor market, employers are struggling to fill vacancies and are increasingly prepared to take risks on younger workers even if they lack the right credentials and have little training or experience,"[1] says Julia Pollak, chief economist for the online career search website ZipRecruiter. The need for employees has created opportunities for youth to enter the workforce, either part time or full time, and work toward their career goals.

> "In an extremely tight labor market, employers are struggling to fill vacancies and are increasingly prepared to take risks on younger workers even if they lack the right credentials and have little training or experience."[1]
>
> —Julia Pollak, chief economist for the online career search website ZipRecruiter

Be Ready

As positive as these developments have been for young workers, it is important to understand that the job market is constantly changing. A slowdown in hiring and a rise in unemployment are always possible. To be in a position where you can still obtain a wanted job, it is important to gain skills and develop traits that employers always need.

Nearly all companies need employees with digital skills, no matter the position. Employers have come to expect that new employees will be able to easily adapt to any technology associated with their job. Additionally, they must be able to learn as the technology develops. "Digital literacy is a broad concept: you can work with digital devices from simple ways to high complex tasks," explains Ying Zhou, director of the Future of Work Research Centre at the University of Surrey in the United Kingdom. "It can vary from printing out an invoice in a shop, to using word processors and spreadsheets, to advanced use like web design, data analysis, computer programming and coding."[2] These types of skills are even expected in roles unrelated to technology. Warehouse operators might need to use a software supply management system, veterinarian assistants might input patient information into tablets, and retail workers might need to use software systems to track inventory.

Additionally, in today's workplace, employees need to be adaptable. Job requirements sometimes change. The most successful employees are those who can adapt to such changes. Job requirements can change for many reasons. One is automation. For example, many grocery stores have installed self-checkout lines. This usually means that fewer employees are needed to work as cashiers or baggers. However, most grocery stores need employees to oversee the self-checkout area. Their duties include helping customers who encounter problems with self-checkout. Learning how the equipment works and how to fix problems that arise for customers could put a former cashier or bagger into a stronger position to fulfil that new job. "The key

A teen works at a concession stand at an amusement park. As a result of the COVID-19 pandemic, many employers began turning to teens and young adults to fill jobs and were willing to pay higher wages for that work.

skill many young people have is the ability to adapt. We may never have been taught how to use a mobile phone, we just picked it up. The same goes for Instagram, Facebook, Snapchat and other social media—at least for some. As soon as the new 'thing' comes along, we'll do just the same,"[3] says James Sancto of We Make Change, a nonprofit organization that helps start-up companies. Being young and able to adapt will allow you to easily learn new skills and technology, and that will help keep you employed and employable.

Up for the Challenge

This holds true even for those with entrepreneurial spirit. Brian Jones, age nineteen, is an example of a young man who has shown the ability to adapt to changing workplace needs. While in high school in Memphis, Tennessee, Jones trained as a barber. When he graduated in 2020, he opened his own barbershop. He built up a client base that included some celebrities and used Instagram to market his business, charging as much as seventy-five dollars a cut. However, as inflation increased, he lost clients who were less willing to pay those prices for haircuts. Almost immediately, Jones came up with an alternate source of income: he started an online barber school. This new venture has brought in needed income until his primary barber business picks up again. His story shows the benefits of perseverance, adaptability, and willingness to learn and try new things.

CHAPTER ONE

What Kind of Job Do You Want?

At some point in life, you realize you want and need a job. You may be fifteen years old and wanting to save up to buy a car or go to college. Or you could be graduating high school and looking for a full-time job so you can live independently. Whatever the reason for wanting a job, the process of finding one begins with determining what you are interested in doing and what skills and abilities you have—or need to develop. While few people land their dream job at the start, this first job can lead in that direction.

This is the path Laura took. She grew up in Ireland, where she developed a love of horses and horse racing. By the time she was in college, she knew she wanted to work in the horse-racing industry, but she needed to develop her skills so that she would have something to offer an employer. She also knew she would have to start at the bottom. While still in college, she got a job mucking out stables and caring for horses. After graduation, she landed a job in Kentucky, known for its connection to horses and horse racing. "My first job as a graduate was as a yearling groom in Kentucky, USA. About three days after finishing my exams, I hopped on a plane and went straight there. It was a massive learning experience for me, and my job essentially was to look after the yearlings and prepare them for the sales in the autumn,"[4] she explains.

A few years later Laura got a job as a racing and communications assistant for a well-known Thoroughbred trainer in England. By 2021 she was working as a client accounts administrator for an organization that develops and promotes horse racing in Ireland. She had finally gotten her dream job—but only after learning as much as she could at low-level jobs and then working her way up.

"My first job as a graduate was as a yearling groom in Kentucky, USA. About three days after finishing my exams, I hopped on a plane and went straight there."[4]

—Laura, racing and communications assistant in the horse-racing industry

What Do You Like?

The first step in any job search is to think about what you like to do. To start, make a list of all the activities you are involved in— both in and out of school. Include volunteer work, sports activities, clubs, and hobbies. Also list the classes that you found most interesting and why. Creating a list like this can help you narrow down your interests, and a little basic research can show you some of the careers that might pair well with the things you like to do. You can then go on career websites and read about different types of careers to see which ones match your interests.

Another way to discover the types of jobs you may like is to take career aptitude tests. These tests ask questions aimed at helping you understand more about yourself, your motivations, and the types of jobs that best match your wants and goals. There are many free, online career tests available such as 123 Career Aptitude Test, which focuses on linking careers to your personality and character traits, or CareerOneStop, which matches a user's skills to suggested careers. And remember that career tests are just a tool to give you ideas. You ultimately decide if the recommended careers interest you.

When completing any type of career test, the key is to answer the questions honestly. "A career test's results will only be as good as the information you put in through your responses,"

This picture shows a woman cleaning or "mucking out" a horse stable. Many people end up in their dream jobs only after starting in low-level jobs such as this and then working their way up.

explains Peter Vogt, a senior contributing writer for the national job search website Monster. "So be honest. Respond in terms of the way you actually are, not the way you hope to be or wish you could be. And make sure the responses are yours, not (subconsciously) those of someone else in your life."[5]

Keep in mind that career aptitude tests are a tool. If the test doesn't reflect your interests, needs, or wants, there's nothing that says you have to follow up on the results. These tests are just another way to identify careers that might suit you.

"A career test's results will only be as good as the information you put in through your responses."[5]

—Peter Vogt, senior contributing writer for Monster, a national job search website

What Are Your Skills?

As you think about what types of jobs to pursue, consider the skills and abilities you already have as well as the ones you would like to develop. Then make a list and do a little research to determine what kinds of jobs require these skills or abilities. For instance, someone who has obtained cardiopulmonary resuscitation (CPR) certification and enjoys helping people might enjoy working at a childcare center, as a lifeguard, or at a summer camp. Someone who likes to work on cars might enjoy working as a mechanic. Computer skills are highly desirable in many career fields, whether they were learned at school or on your own. Even skills gained from computer gaming can be included on this list. Skills learned through volunteer work, hobbies, and other activities should also make the list. This type of information can be valuable when looking for summer jobs or when thinking about long-term career goals.

You also should consider what classes you excel in at school. Whether you are attending high school, college, or a vocational school, your classes can help you determine your strengths and interests. Someone who excels in math might want to consider

Military Career Test

The US military has its own career aptitude test. It's known as the Armed Services Vocational Aptitude Battery (ASVAB). All military applicants take the test. It is also offered to high school and postsecondary students who are considering joining the military or who just want to know where their strengths lie. "It's a good test to take, just in general, when you're 17, you don't know what you want to do. This shows you what you're good at," says Cindy Covarrubias, a veteran of US Army intelligence.

The test consists of nine subtests in categories such as word knowledge, arithmetic reasoning, and mechanical comprehension. It lasts about two and a half hours. Once the test has been completed, the scores are analyzed. A high score in arithmetic reasoning might lead to a suggested career in cryptology. A strong score in paragraph comprehension and word knowledge might lead to a suggested career in public affairs. When assigning a career path to a new member of the military, the military branches consider requested careers, ASVAB scores, and what areas need service personnel.

Quoted in Bret Anne Serbin, "Army Vet Teaches Military Prep Course at FPVCC," Yahoo! News, August 30, 2021. https://news.yahoo.com.

teaching or engineering. Someone who excels at languages might want to consider careers in public administration or international business. Someone who excels in science can investigate a wide variety of science-oriented careers—some that involve research and others that involve working directly with people. Understanding both what you like and what you are skilled at will lead you toward jobs that are well suited to you.

Why Do You Need a Job?

People look for jobs at different stages of their lives and for different reasons. A high school student might want a summer job to get workplace experience and earn some extra money or to help with family finances. A college student who is paying for school and supporting himself or herself might need a full-time job but with flexible hours. Considering your personal needs is one more way to guide a job search.

Those who have to support themselves will probably want to look for a full-time job that pays enough to live on. Ideally, that job

One way to figure out what type of career you might like is to take an online career test. These tests ask questions aimed at helping you understand more about yourself, your motivations, and the types of jobs that might match your wants and goals.

Age Limits

Young people applying for jobs need to be aware of age limits. The Fair Labor Standards Act (FLSA) sets fourteen years old as the minimum age for working in most jobs. This law also limits how many hours someone under age sixteen can work. There are other limitations based on age. The FLSA prohibits minors from working in jobs that require driving or operating power-driven equipment. Other limits include working in a restaurant that serves alcohol or at a bar. You cannot serve alcohol or work as a bartender in any state if you are under age eighteen.

However, age is not a factor in all jobs. Minors can work as performers in television, movies, and theater. They can work in businesses owned by their parents. They can also find work babysitting, walking dogs, or helping with household or other chores.

will come with benefits such as employer-sponsored group health insurance, sick leave, vacation days, and a 401(k) retirement plan. While employees often pay for some part of their health insurance, a company-sponsored plan can greatly reduce costs of doctor visits and hospital stays.

Sometimes people get jobs with an eye toward saving money for something specific. This might be a high school student who wants to buy a car, get a new laptop, or help with college costs after graduation. For this purpose, a part-time job that allows you to work after school or on weekends might be a good option.

Another reason teens and young adults look for jobs is to obtain skills or experience for a future career. Paid internships are a way to gain workplace experience. Summer jobs can do the same. For example, a teen or young adult who wants to be a teacher can gain real-world experience working as a tutor or possibly even as a camp counselor. Your reason for finding a job will lead you to one that will help to accomplish your objectives.

Logistics of the Job

In addition to your likes, skills, and reasons for wanting to work, it's important to be clear on your schedule, location, and workplace needs. Being offered your dream job in California would not work if you have absolutely no interest in leaving your home in the

Midwest. Similarly, why spend time look for a high-paying, forty-hour-a-week job if you are a full-time student and can only work twenty hours a week? A further consideration in your job search is whether you want a job that enables you to work on-site, remotely, or in a hybrid arrangement with some days at home and other days in the office.

If you do not determine your logistical requirements before a job search, you may find yourself in a job that does not work for your lifestyle. For example, sometimes people start a new job and then discover the commute is too long. Other times people find that a new job requires more hours than they want to work. You can narrow your job search by determining your logistical needs ahead of time so this does not happen to you.

All Together

Remember that discovering what type of job is right for you is not always a straightforward path. For example, Tasha Hayes went to college with the goal of one day becoming a surgeon. A few years into her coursework, she realized that this was not what she wanted to do. Today she organizes and manages adventure travel

This picture shows freeway traffic in the San Francisco Bay Area. Before starting a job search, it is important to determine your logistical requirements, such as whether you can handle a long daily commute.

trips for eighteen-to-thirty-five-year-olds—and she loves her job. Hayes explains:

> From as far back as I can remember I wanted to be a surgeon. But after struggling through organic chemistry in my second year of university, I realized it wasn't the path for me. I took a Geography class to fulfil a general education requirement and absolutely loved it! I found myself signing up for more geography and global studies classes until I finally decided that was the path for me.[6]

Hayes graduated with degrees in geography and global studies from Binghamton University in New York. After graduation, she planned and took a six-week trip in Europe. She realized her organizational skills combined with her world knowledge were leading her toward a career in adventure travel. She knew she wanted full-time work, was open to living outside the United States, and wanted a job that allowed her to travel. Once her trip was over, she applied for a job as a European trip manager for an adventure travel company based in the United Kingdom. After several interviews, Hayes got the job, flew to London, and trained for two months as she traveled with the company. "I spent the next three or so years taking keen young travelers around Europe and teaching them about the local cultures and histories,"[7] says Hayes. She has continued to work for the same company but has been promoted to a position as a European operations manager.

"I took a Geography class to fulfil a general education requirement and absolutely loved it! I found myself signing up for more geography and global studies classes until I finally decided that was the path for me."[6]

—Tasha Hayes, European operations manager for an adventure travel company

Hayes discovered her career path as she considered what she loved to do, her knowledge of the world, her organizational skills, and her willingness to live and work in another country. Considering your wants and needs will help lead you to the right job—even if it takes a circuitous route.

CHAPTER TWO

Preparation

It can take a lot of time and energy to look for a job. Those who prepare ahead of time are less likely to waste precious time and energy and more likely to get the job they want.

Essential Résumés

Résumés are still essential to obtaining a job. A résumé provides a company with its first look at you. You want a résumé that stands out and represents you.

To begin, you should know the general résumé format, but understand there are different formats that you can review on résumé websites. There are many online free sites that have set formats you can download and follow. In nearly all formats, your name, address, phone number, and email address will appear at the top of the résumé. The remainder of the résumé is usually divided into sections that describe your work experience, skills, education, awards and certifications (if any), and sometimes other interests.

Some résumés start with the heading "Summary" or "Objective." This section usually consists of one to two sentences that state your skills or accomplishments and/or what sort of job you hope to get. This section serves as a hook to get a manager interested in you. Focus on including your most relevant skills. Typical sections in the résumé include the following:

- **Work Experience** (prior jobs with dates and brief descriptions of your responsibilities and achievements)
- **Education** (schooling to date; year of graduation, if applicable; and any academic honors)
- **Skills** (certifications or special skills, such as CPR training or fluency in a foreign language)
- **Volunteer Work** or **Other Interests** (other activities that provide additional information about you that might interest a potential employer)

These sections can be adapted to your personal circumstances. For instance, if you are a high school student who doesn't have a lot of work experience but have volunteer experience, you might want to combine those two topics under the heading "Job and Volunteer Experience." In the descriptions, you would clearly identify which listings are volunteer work and which are jobs. Either way, all of this constitutes experience that would interest a potential employer.

What to Include

Determining which format to use for a résumé and setting that up is an easy process to follow due to all of the online resources. Often, websites include résumé builders, where you just input the information and the software builds the résumé. This can help ensure your layout, font, and margins remain consistent throughout the résumé.

However, deciding what to include in your résumé and how to describe your background are what will be key to getting your résumé noticed. First, you must consider the algorithms that are used to review résumés on companies' job submission sites and other online job applications. Algorithms (which are computer programs) usually get first crack at résumés uploaded to job search or company websites. Having the right keywords on a résumé is crucial to getting past the algorithm gatekeeper. A résumé that passes that first test will likely end up in the hands of a real person, although that person will probably just glance at it to decide whether to send it on to the hiring manager. So what you include on your résumé and how you include it really matter. According to Sulaiman Rahman, CEO of the job recruiting company DiverseForce, "Organizations are increasingly using automation to screen resumes, so it's important for job seekers to use keywords that are also found in the actual job description."[8] If the résumé does not include some or even most of the keywords, it likely will not get to a recruiter or any person in the company for a review.

It is usually easy to find important keywords in job postings. For instance, if the job description states that applicants need to know the Java programming language and you've taken a course or have a certificate in Java, make sure to include this in your résumé. Or if the job description states that the candidate

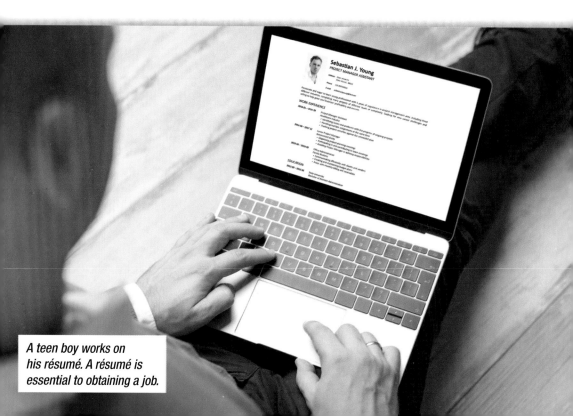

A teen boy works on his résumé. A résumé is essential to obtaining a job.

Social Media Presence

An important preparation for a job search is to ensure you have a clean social media presence. This means it would be best if your public social media presence does not include pictures of you drunk or partying, cursing in posts, or posting racist or other discriminatory remarks. While you have the right to post what you want, if your social media accounts are public, recruiters and potential employers can and do look at the social media of applicants. According to a 2020 poll by the business information company Manifest, 90 percent of employers believe social media is important when they consider candidates. Additionally, 79 percent of human resources professionals have denied a job to a candidate due to inappropriate content on social media. The takeaway: think twice before posting that selfie from a party.

must be able to work well with others, try to include something that shows you collaborating with others on a project or working with others to organize an event.

Keep in mind that you might have to make changes in your résumé for each job that you apply to. Use the keywords in each job posting as your guide. But always make sure that you are being truthful. Nothing good comes of falsifying a résumé. If the job has too many requirements that don't apply to you, consider applying for a different job.

Past the Algorithm

Once past the algorithm, your résumé still needs to catch a recruiter or company reviewer's eye. Kristi DePaul, founder and CEO of the marketing agency Founders Marketing, often writes and speaks about the future of the workplace. She writes:

> How long does it take a recruiter to decide if you're right for a job? It's actually around seven seconds, according to eye-tracking research. To put that into perspective, close your eyes and take two deep breaths. That's the time, on average, hiring managers spend skimming your resume, sizing up your history, hopes, and dreams before either tossing it into the trash or moving you to the next round of the application process.[9]

With this in mind, it is important to find ways to make your résumé stand out. Where possible, include numbers. If you helped organize an event, show how many people were involved in organizing and attending the event. If you helped raise money for a cause, include how much money was raised. Include major projects or accomplishments at previous jobs, volunteer work, or classes in your experience section. Emphasize anything that shows time-management skills, such as meeting deadlines, and communication skills, both written and verbal.

At just eighteen years old and a freshman in college, Ahmed Ishaque applied for a coveted position as a paid intern at Google. He had no related work experience, and he was competing with students who were further along in their education. Even so, Ishaque got the job. He believes it was his résumé that got him in the door for interviews. Ishaque says:

> My resume didn't have any work experience related to Software Engineering, so I had to craft it carefully. I made sure to include any relevant Computer Science coursework I had taken or was currently taking under the "Education" section. I also made sure to add a section titled "Projects" to highlight the programming projects I had made. This demonstrated my ability to code and which languages I had experience in. Both of these things were very important, and I believe they are what allowed me to get past the resume screening round.[10]

Cover Letter

Before the days of uploaded résumés, job applicants nearly always submitted a cover letter with their résumé. Cover letters

20

are a way to let an employer know why you want the job and why you are a good match for it. Many companies still want to see cover letters. This is supported by the results of a 2022 poll of two hundred job recruiters, human resources specialists, and hiring managers. In that poll, 77 percent of respondents said they give preference to candidates who send a cover letter even when a cover letter is not required.

Cover letters are a good way to quickly sell who you are and spark interest in the employer. As with résumés, there are many websites that provide free examples or templates. That being said, it's important to personalize the letter so that it shows a potential employer something relevant about you.

Cover letters generally consist of three paragraphs. They should not exceed one page. At the top is a heading that matches the heading of your résumé. Your opening should be to a specific person if you know who will be receiving your cover letter or to a title, such as human resources director, if not. The first paragraph should be about why you are applying for the specific job and company. In the second paragraph, you want to show why

Paid or unpaid internships, such as those sometimes offered at Google, can lead to future employment due to gained work experience.

you are a good choice for the job. This should include your major qualifications, education, and experience, and how they match the job requirements. The last paragraph is a way to close the letter. Express that you hope to hear from them and thank them for considering you. Lastly, include a closing with "Sincerely," followed by your name.

This is a business letter, so keep the tone simple and formal, but show your personality through word choices and expressions. The cover letter should be formatted in the same font and type size as the résumé. Always reread your letter and résumé to make sure

When starting a job search it can be helpful to reach out to teachers and other people you know and let them know you are looking for a job.

Video Résumé Boom

Today a different type of résumé is being used by some job applicants as a way to stand out from the crowd. These individuals are creating video résumés that can be uploaded to job search and company websites. Some companies have started requesting video résumés for certain jobs. Even when not required, some applicants choose to submit video résumés along with their written résumé in hopes of gaining the attention of the company.

Online platforms have responded to this trend. LinkedIn gives users the ability to upload a thirty-second video to their profile. The video gives them another way to introduce themselves and call attention to their skills, interests, and experience. TikTok, the wildly popular app known for short videos, has also gotten involved. In 2021 it created "TikTok Resumes," a program that allows users to upload brief video résumés that can be reviewed by employers.

there are no spelling errors or grammatical mistakes, as that would give a poor first impression. A well-formatted résumé and cover letter with compelling content just might get you that first interview.

References

In addition to a cover letter and résumé, it is important to have references ready before applying for jobs. Often jobs will require you to submit references during the application process or will ask for them if you make it past the first stage. References are people employers may contact to get information on your work experience, character traits, work ethic, and skills.

When choosing a reference, do not ask family or friends. They will not be considered reliable references by recruiters and employers. Choose people who have positive views of your habits, skills, and personality. Examples of good choices are previous bosses, teachers, professors, pastors, clients, and work or volunteer supervisors or colleagues. Always check first with the people you want to use as references to make sure they are willing to speak your praises and also to get their correct email address and phone number. These references might provide the edge needed to get the job.

Meeting People

Lastly, as you are preparing your résumé and cover letter and obtaining references, it is important to reach out to people and let them know you are beginning a job search. This can include friends, teachers and professors, members of clubs you are active in, leaders of organizations you volunteer with, or anyone you know who works in a career field or job that interests you. The more people who know of your job search, the greater the chance that someone will hear of an opening and pass that information along.

Once you've accomplished all of these, it is time to move on to actually applying for jobs. If you've followed the preparation process carefully, you should be ready to take active steps toward getting hired.

CHAPTER THREE

Search and Apply

Once you've finished preparations and your résumé is ready to go, it is time to start searching and applying for jobs. This process can feel like a full-time job—and that's because it is. It takes a lot of time, effort, and perseverance. Schedule a portion of time each day to search, apply, track, and follow up on job applications. Be prepared for rejection, since it happens, but do not let that stop you from persevering. You will find a job that will help you achieve your goals. The key is to be patient and keep searching.

Fire Up Your Contacts

While preparing for the job search, you connected with people in your clubs, school, volunteer organizations, sports, and online groups. Now it is time to check in with them on a periodic basis to see if they have heard of any available jobs suited for you. Additionally, politely ask them to spread your name to potential employers if they believe you could be a good fit with those companies. If they do give you potential job contacts, when calling or emailing the contact, make sure to mention the person who referred you. This way you have a personal contact when applying for a job. From there, if there is a job opening, apply and make sure you also include who referred you in your cover letter.

It was through a contact that Melissa MacCoubrey landed her first job as a video game script-writing intern with Ubisoft Montreal. In this job, she worked with the head of script writing, reading the scripts of video games and providing feedback to the game writers. MacCoubrey had studied drama and English literature at Bishop's University in Quebec, and her playwriting professor introduced her to a person who worked in scripts at the Ubisoft Montreal studio. MacCoubrey says:

> I gave [the Ubisoft contact] a binder of everything I'd ever done in my creative life and asked him to let me know if anyone ever needed any help. A few months later, he got in contact about a potential internship opening, and asked if I could write a screenplay to submit with my other writing samples. Having never written a screenplay in my life, I, of course, said "absolutely!" and spent the next two days looking at examples of screenplay formatting and writing my own twenty-page submission.[11]

MacCoubrey submitted her work, was asked to interview, and was hired, having started the process from her professor's introduction.

How to Search

As you begin your search, ensure you set up a way to track all of the potential jobs that you are pursuing. Create a spreadsheet on Excel or another tracking software and include the status of all job applications. On this spreadsheet you want to track the company, job position, where you found the job (such as in person at a store or on career website), phone number, point of contact if you have one, when you submitted your résumé and cover letter, and the status—rejected, interview scheduled, and offer made. Update this spreadsheet daily to keep yourself on track.

"I asked [my professor] to let me know if anyone ever needed any help. A few months later, he got in contact about a potential internship opening, and asked if I could write a screenplay to submit with my other writing samples."[11]

—Melissa MacCoubrey, video game scriptwriting intern with Ubisoft Montreal

26

When you are looking for a job, you should schedule a portion of each day to search, apply, track, and follow up on job applications.

Searching for jobs online will likely be your most common search method. There are numerous online job search sites that list thousands of posted job descriptions from companies in different career fields. Users can narrow the jobs they view by setting filters on the search in order to find jobs that interest them. Additionally, there are career sites with a narrow focus, listing only posted jobs in select career fields, such as sports and recreation or marketing. If you know you are interested in a specific field, these sites can help you target jobs in that field.

No matter what career site you visit, all of them allow you to upload a résumé and apply for specific positions. Many of the online job sites also allow job seekers to create a profile that potential employers can view when they have openings. You provide specific information about yourself, upload your résumé in a profile, and choose an option that allows employers to view it. This means your résumé can be seen even if you have not applied for their specific job, and they will be able to contact you.

Before getting started on these websites, decide the parameters of your job search, such as location and whether you're looking for a full-time or part-time position. Typically, these websites allow you to narrow your search using these and other filters and by typing in keywords. You can also arrange for the websites to send you emails when they receive job postings that match your parameters.

LinkedIn

With more than 850 million users as of 2022, LinkedIn is one of the most popular online tools used for a job search. Job seekers can find all sorts of posted job openings on the site. However, its most important feature is as a professional networking site where people with similar professional interests can connect with one another. Users create profiles, post résumés, and link to other people in similar professions or in career fields that interest them. What might start out as a small network of linked professionals can grow to include many others who share the same professional interests. Through this expanded network of mutual connections, people often learn of job openings they might have missed or companies that might be of interest in the future.

LinkedIn proved to be a useful tool in Josh Gwin's job search. On the site, he saw that a nationwide automotive technology com-

How to Stay Positive

"It's easy to become tired of writing cover letters, going to interviews, and networking. However, try to think of each activity as an opportunity that will only make you a better candidate. If you are interviewing for a job you don't think you want (or don't think you will get), try to think of the interview as a chance to network and to work on your interview skills. Think of each cover letter as the chance to hone your writing and editing abilities. Simply thinking of tasks as opportunities rather than chores will put you in a positive mindset."

—Big Jobs Today

Big Jobs Today, "How to Stay Positive During a Job Search," July 21, 2021. https://bdjobstoday.org.

pany he was interested in had posted a job for a sales and marketing consultant. He then searched LinkedIn and found that there was a vice president at the company with whom he had mutual connections. He sent a connection request to this vice president with a personalized message that he was interested in the job. In the message, Gwin asked whether there was someone to whom he could send his résumé directly. "[The vice president] said to send it to him and he would forward it along to the hiring manager," Gwin writes. "Within a week or so I got a call about interviewing with the hiring manager. Had one phone interview, one in-person interview, got the job with a $5 billion tech company."[12]

> "[The vice president] said to send [my résumé] to him and he would forward it along to the hiring manager. Within a week or so I got a call about interviewing with the hiring manager. Had one phone interview, one in-person interview, got the job with a $5 billion tech company."[12]
>
> —Josh Gwin, automotive technology consultant

Company Websites

The job search websites are a type of one-stop shop for people looking for work, but they are not the only option. Many businesses post their job openings on their websites. Job seekers who have a particular company in mind can search those posts and apply directly to the company. Not all businesses use an applicant tracking system (ATS), which relies on algorithms to prescreen résumés. This means that a job seeker's résumé might go directly to human resources or a hiring manager. Amanda Augustine, a career advice expert for the résumé writing service TopResume, explains:

> If the company does not use ATS software to manage its recruitment process, you may have the luxury of forgoing the robotic application pre-screen when you apply directly to their listings. Since these systems often eliminate great candidates, whose resumes aren't formatted or written with this technological gatekeeper in mind, your candidacy may be more likely to be considered for the position.[13]

World's Largest Profession

https://www.linkedin.com

Linked in.

Connect, share ideas, and di

LinkedIn is a popular site for online job searching. It can also be useful as a professional networking site.

Once you've found a job on your search, then it is time to click "Apply." Typically, you will be asked to submit a résumé and cover letter. Ensure that you submit a version of your résumé that is best suited for the particular job. You will likely also have to fill out a job application with work history, education, and other basic information about yourself. Once you have done this, add the job to your spreadsheet, and then continue searching for more job opportunities.

In Person

While most job applications are online, there are still jobs for which you can apply in person. One way to find out is to walk or drive through town or visit the mall to see if there are any Help Wanted or We're Hiring signs. In-person applications are most likely to involve retail and restaurant jobs. Make a list of the places that interest you so that you can return later that day or another day. Showing up in shorts and flip-flops or stained jeans to apply for a job will not make a good first impression.

When you're ready to apply for these jobs, dress neatly, comb your hair, and then head to the business with a résumé, cover letter, and pen. Also have a current driver's license or other form of ID. When on-site, ask to speak with a manager and tell him or her that you would like to apply for a job.

Whether meeting the manager or speaking to an employee, extend your hand for a handshake and introduce yourself. You may then be given a paper application to complete. Also, you may be asked to fill out an application at a kiosk. Retail stores such as Target and Walmart often use hiring kiosks, where potential employees complete an electronic version of a job application. In either case, fill out the application carefully and accurately, ensuring that you do not make any spelling, grammatical, or factual mistakes.

College Job Fairs

Once you reach college, be on the lookout for college job fairs. Most colleges have them. Job fairs are an opportunity for students to learn about job prospects at various businesses and to meet individuals who work for them.

If you go to a job fair, arrive prepared. Come up with a few good questions to ask each representative. Dress for success, speak with confidence, shake hands when introducing yourself, and show your enthusiasm. Bring résumés to provide to company representatives, and ask for business cards.

After, there is still an important step. Mike Profita, director of career services at Skidmore College for twenty-four years, comments on the importance of following up:

> Effective follow-up after the program will be essential for moving your employment prospects forward. Make sure you get the contact information for any of the interesting recruiters with whom you have met. As soon as possible after you leave the event, compose a communication to them which briefly conveys why the firm is an excellent fit given your background. Make sure that you communicate a strong sense of your interest in a future meeting with the organization to further explore opportunities.

Mike Profita, "Tips for Attending a College Job Fair," University of Mary Washington, 2022. www.umw.edu.

Once you have completed the application, turn it in and thank the person. Offer your résumé and cover letter for the person to review as well. Show a positive attitude and let him or her know you are excited about the potential opportunity.

Follow-Up

Whether you apply in person or online, try to follow up on your applications. Following up is not always easy since, with online applications, you may not have a phone number or specific person to contact. A little online research might lead you to the company's human resources department or even to a manager you could contact. If not, you still can probably find a general number for the business.

A business owner puts up a "help wanted" sign. Looking for help wanted signs is one way to find job opportunities.

About a week after applying, call the number you have and either ask to speak to a specific person, if you know who is in charge of hiring or if you interacted with anyone during the application process, or ask for the human resources department. Whether you get to a live person or a voice mail, politely say who you are, what position you applied for and when, and that you are excited about the potential opportunity and are checking in to see if there is an updated status or if they require more information. If leaving a message, ensure you leave your phone number.

During this part of the job search process, your days will likely include calling or emailing your contacts, searching for jobs, applying online for jobs, following up on jobs you've applied for, and updating your status on your spreadsheet. While it can get monotonous and even discouraging, remember that there's a good chance that all of this work will result in the right job for you.

CHAPTER FOUR

Time for an Interview

It finally happened! You got an email, text, or phone call from a company that wants you to interview for a position. Getting an interview is an exciting, major step in the job search. It is typically your first chance to show yourself, in person, to a company. Don't wing it. The first rule of job interviews is to go prepared. Prepare how you will dress, practice talking and answering questions, and learn a little about the company. Some job candidates go through only one interview. Others have multiple interviews. Sometimes interviews are conducted by one person. Other times interviews are conducted by a panel of people. You may not know until the actual interview what the situation is, so be prepared and confident.

Preparation

Many businesses describe their origins, mission, and goals on their website. Before going to an interview, read up on the company and the position you've applied for. Understand the specifics of the job—what duties it entails, what skills and background the company wants you to have, and any other available information. Know all of this well so that whoever interviews you knows that you have a thorough understanding of what the company wants from someone in this position. That way you can explain how you, personally, are a good fit.

Before going to the interview, practice answering questions out loud. Most job interviews include general questions such as why you are interested in the job, what your

34

strengths and weaknesses are, and what makes you stand out compared to other applicants. A Starbucks employee, who was hired at age sixteen, recalls his interview process. He was asked to interview after the company reviewed his job application and references, which he had provided in person. He explains:

> The actual interview was regular interview style. You come in, talk to the hiring manager. "Why do you want to work here?," "What time are you available?," "Where have you worked before?," "Can I call previous managers?," "What goals and skills do you have that can better your experience here?," "What skills do you have that can improve the work area?," "What can you offer?," "Why should we take you in?," "Why should we employ you?," just basic stuff like that.[14]

He received the job shortly after he completed the interview.

Management jobs and jobs requiring specific skills, such as welding or coding, will likely include more specific questions. Ahmed Ishaque applied to Google for a position as a software engineering intern. After getting selected for an interview, Ishaque

A young woman talks during a job interview. Getting an interview is an exciting step in the job search process.

knew the questions would be technical, so he practiced. "The recruiter told me that the interview would be technical, so I had to sharpen up my coding and problem solving skills. As soon as my Winter Break started, I practiced questions on LeetCode.com and did mock interviews with a friend every day to help me get used to thinking out loud while coding," Ishaque writes. "After two weeks of intense preparation, it was time for the big day."[15] The preparation was successful. Ishaque interviewed with two separate people via phone on the same day, and just over a month later, Google offered him the job.

Anxiety and Attitude

Before you go to your interview, eat a good breakfast or lunch so you are not hungry during the interview. Take a walk, do yoga, or exercise to calm your nerves. As you get ready, listen to music or a podcast or watch a TV show to de-stress.

What They Cannot Ask

Under state and federal laws, there are many questions that interviewers cannot ask applicants during job interviews. In most cases questions about your age, race, sex, national origin, religion, family status, and disability are not allowed. The laws that prohibit questions on these topics are aimed at protecting potential employees from discrimination.

However, some jobs have specific requirements that affect the person's ability to do the work. In these cases questions on some of these topics might be allowed. For instance, airline pilots have specific age requirements, so questions about age are allowed. Another example is for certain jobs at religious schools. For example, a prospective teacher can be asked about his or her religious beliefs if being hired to teach religion or theology.

If you are asked a question that is not allowed and you do not want to answer, say something about this to the interviewer in a polite but firm way. If he or she does not respond well, you have the right to bring that up to higher-level managers in the company.

Before you go to your job interview, do something to calm your nerves, such as exercise or yoga.

Whether the interview is in person or virtual, ensure you are dressed appropriately. Do not dress casually, such as in jeans and a T-shirt. For an office job interview, a business suit is appropriate. For retail stores and restaurants, dressy casual is fine. In addition to dressing well, remember to bring copies of your résumé, identification, and Social Security number.

One of the most important "musts" is to show up on time. Give yourself plenty of time to arrive at your interview. If you are driving to the interview, account for traffic. If you are calling or connecting virtually, ensure you are by your phone and in a quiet place at least ten minutes before the scheduled call. Showing up late leaves the impression that you do not care enough about the job or have the appropriate work ethic.

Interviewers consider not only what you say but how you conduct yourself and your attitude. Be positive, friendly, and enthusiastic. Introduce yourself and shake hands with anyone you meet. "Degrees and credentials won't carry much weight if the hiring manager thinks you're defensive, moody, arrogant, unmotivated, insecure or uncooperative. When preparing for a job interview, decide how you want to be perceived and act accordingly through your dress, body language and thoughtful responses

Learn from Your Experiences

You might have a difficult interview. It happens. You might get overly nervous. The job could be something different than you expected, and you do not have the appropriate skills. Or you just don't connect with the interviewer. In a 2021 BuzzFeed article about people's worst job interviews, one anonymous writer tells the story of an interview that went from bad to worse. "The interviewer was just stone cold. I tried to work in some small chitchat to break the ice, but the most I got was a smirk. . . . Then came the technical questions. I botched every question, and each time he gave me a hard 'no,' then proceeded to condescendingly explain why I was wrong. Luckily, I landed a job with a different company shortly after, but man that interview really destroyed my confidence."

If you have a bad interview, do not despair. Learn what you could have done better or different and chalk it up to experience.

Quoted in Brian Galindo, "People Are Sharing the Worst Job Interview Experience They Ever Had, and I Truly Would Have Walked Out on Most of These," BuzzFeed, May 9, 2021. www.buzzfeed.com.

to questions that probe your underlying beliefs and attitudes,"[16] writes Mary Dowd, a reporter on careers for Chron, a Houston daily online news source.

Even with preparation, most people feel anxious about job interviews. Being nervous is normal, but there are ways to calm your nerves. Alyse Kalish, a seasoned writer on career topics for the Muse, suggests using the STOP method developed by executive coach Chris Charyk. Kalish explains:

> Stop what you're doing and focus on your thoughts. Take a few deep breaths. Observe what's going on in your body, emotions, and mind, and why you're feeling them. Proceed with an intention to incorporate what you observed in your actions. The importance of this technique is to slow down and be deliberate not just in the things you do, but the feelings you let take over. It reminds you that you have the power to banish your own fears, doubts, and nerves in even the most pressure-cooker situations.[17]

Asking Questions

At the end of the interview, you will almost always be asked whether you have any questions. It is important to have questions ready to ask. These should not be about salary or hours, unless you have been offered the job, but about the position itself and the company. Examples of good questions to ask include: What does a typical day look like in the role? What are some of the biggest challenges this job includes? What attributes does a person need to be successful in this role? Good questions show thoughtfulness and interest in the company.

Additionally, ask each person you interview with for a business card. This way you will be able to remember who you met and send them a thank-you later. Before you leave, restate your interest in the job and why you would make a good fit. Shake hands and thank the interviewer. Then, you've successfully conducted an interview.

What Not to Do

While there is much you should do during an interview, there is also much you should not do. For one, do not lie. Do not lie on your résumé, and do not lie during an interview. Lies in either case are grounds for immediate dismissal. If you feel you must lie to qualify for the job, then the job is not right for you.

Since you want to show that you are interested in the job and company, make sure you do not look bored. Specifically, do not check your phone—at all—while at the interview. Before you walk into the room or enter the virtual space, turn off your phone and put it away. Checking your phone while being interviewed tells the employer you aren't really all that interested in the job.

While it is good to show that you have confidence in yourself, do not act cocky, and do not give the impression that you think the job would be easy or unchallenging. Even if you've done similar work before, every business runs differently. New employees, regardless of their experience, always have a lot to learn. Additionally, do not get overly familiar with the interviewer. Even if you establish a good conversation and connection, you do not want to talk to the interviewer as if he or she were a friend. "Be polite, but never become too familiar," explains Jodi Chavez, president of the staffing agency Randstad USA Professionals, Life Sciences & Tatum. "Many people assume comfort early on in an attempt to build rapport, but this could put off your interviewer."[18]

Virtual Interview

Virtual interviews also require preparation. Begin by making sure you have the platform specified by the company. Whether it is Microsoft Teams, Zoom, or another, practice using it beforehand. Set up a meeting on it with a friend to ensure you've got the technology down. Writers for *Harvard Business Review* looked at 513 video recordings of virtual interviews done during March through November 2020. They found that 41 percent of those interviews experienced disruptions related to technology. In one interview, for example, the job candidate appeared upside down on the screen the entire time. Disruptions like this can usually be

This picture shows a virtual job interview. Virtual interviews have become increasingly common.

prevented, or at least fixed, if the individual being interviewed has experimented with the platform ahead of time.

Ensure that you have an appropriate background, both in terms of noise and appearance. Sitting on your patio as cars drive by is not conducive to a good conversation. You need a quiet spot, both to hear and be heard. Likewise, sitting in your bedroom with a poster of your favorite band behind you does not look professional. "Just find a spot that is simple and free of distractions (like a blank wall or one that has a few pictures hanging on it). If your background is too cluttered, it will pull the recruiters attention away from you. You can even choose a simple virtual background instead of propping yourself in front of a messy bookshelf,"[19] a *Harvard Business Review* article suggests.

> "Just find a spot that is simple and free of distractions (like a blank wall or one that has a few pictures hanging on it). If your background is too cluttered, it will pull the recruiters attention away from you. You can even choose a simple virtual background instead of propping yourself in front of a messy bookshelf."[19]
>
> —Writers for *Harvard Business Review*

No matter how good your technology is, remember that virtual interviews might not translate as well as in-person interviews. Always try to speak up and speak clearly. Pay close attention to the person who is speaking or asking questions. When it comes to attitude and answering questions, the rules are the same for virtual interviews as they are for in-person interviews. As in any type of interview, you want to show who you are, why you are well suited for the job, and that you are excited about it.

Follow-Up

After the interview, whether it was in person or online, it is important to follow up. Within a few days, call or send an email to the people you met and thank them for their time and the opportunity. Then, as you wait to hear back, update your spreadsheet and move on to the next tasks in your job search. Remember, no matter what the result, you gained experience in interviewing and got contacts in a company. Eventually, an interview will lead to a job.

CHAPTER FIVE

An Offer and a Job

Elsa Scola remembers well the day she got a job offer to work as a front-end engineer for Amazon in Madrid, Spain. She writes:

> When I first got the offer, I couldn't process it. I hadn't even graduated from college, and I was just being offered to work at this giant company that was already part of my day to day life. To make it clear, I'm a Prime member, Alexa's #1 fan, and . . . it took me a moment to realize how great of an opportunity this was, not only on a professional level (which is obvious), but in terms of the kind of impact that I could have.[20]

Responding to an Offer

Whether a job offer comes by phone, in person, or via email, it is exciting and a reason to feel proud. However, you do not have to accept or decline immediately. It is perfectly acceptable to ask about pay and benefits, hours, start date, and other details that haven't been discussed up to this point. It is also okay to request a couple days to think about it.

But before you start asking questions, be sure to thank the person for the opportunity to work for the company. Make sure you sound appreciative and enthusiastic about the job. "Once you receive a job offer, show the prospective employer that you are excited about the position," recommends the editorial staff at the job search website Indeed.

"How you respond to the offer will reveal your nature as an employee and lay the foundation for the development of your relationship with your new employer."[21]

Once you've thanked the person, you can tell him or her that you have a few questions. It is important to get the details of the job offer. You'll want to ask about pay and benefits and also when the employer expects you to start. Other common questions include: What hours does the employer want you to work? If it is a remote work position, what arrangements does the employer make for remote workers? You can also ask whether there is any training for the job and, if so, what it entails.

Ask for the details of the job offer to be emailed to you. This ensures that both you and the employer are on the same page as far as what is being offered to you. After hearing the details, some people decide to accept the job offer immediately—and that's okay. It's also okay to tell the employer that you'd like to review the details or think about the offer. If you decide to do that, make sure to ask when he or she needs an answer.

> "Once you receive a job offer, show the prospective employer that you are excited about the position."[21]
>
> —Editorial staff at Indeed, a job search website

Receiving a job offer is a reason to feel proud and excited. However, it is acceptable to take time to think about the offer or to ask more questions.

Give Yourself Time

There are many legitimate reasons for not immediately accepting a job offer. You might be considering more than one job offer. You might have other interviews scheduled for jobs that interest you as much or more than this one. Or you may need to think about whether the hours will work or the pay and benefits meet your needs or expectations.

If you are excited about the job itself but are not satisfied with the salary, benefits, hours, or anything the employer has offered, you can consider negotiation. However, this is dependent on the kind of job you are applying for. A no-experience-needed job, such as at a fast-food restaurant or a store, will likely have a set rate per hour, with no negotiation. You can certainly ask, but when offering entry-level jobs, companies are often firm on their pay and benefits. However, the employer may be amenable to negotiating your hours and days of work.

Other jobs may be open to negotiating the terms. You can start negotiating with just a verbal offer of the job and what it

What Day Will I Get a Job?

Once you've interviewed for a job, you may be on edge, waiting for a call or email. Studies have been conducted to show what days hiring managers are most likely to offer jobs. Monday is usually a catch-up day, when managers are completing tasks from the prior week. Jeff Kartheiser, a hiring manager, writes:

> By Tuesday, the tasks that spilled over from the prior week have been completed, and the hiring manager has time to extend an official offer letter. Tuesday is also a popular day to extend offers because it gives the candidate time to review the offer, ask questions and possibly make a counteroffer in the same week. All questions and concerns can be ironed out during the remainder of the week, and the candidate can sign their offer letter by Friday, if not sooner.

So, if you have interviewed at a company, circle the next Tuesday on your calendar, and see what happens.

Editors, "What Time of the Day and Day of the Week Are Job Offers Usually Made?," UpJourney, January 10, 2020. https://upjourney.com.

It can be a good idea to ask for the details of a job offer to be emailed to you so that you can review them in detail before accepting or declining a position.

includes. Or you can wait until you've reviewed the offer in writing. Either way, think about what you want compared to what the employer is offering, and get ready to negotiate.

Negotiation

At its simplest, negotiation is a discussion between two or more parties with the goal of reaching some sort of agreement. "When you do receive a job offer, just know it's not set in stone. If there are certain things that you don't like about your offer, you can negotiate those details,"[22] writes Kristen Winiarski, who specializes in writing about human resources and career advice. But first it's important to decide what you want to negotiate. Just about everything—salary, work schedule, health plan, days off—is negotiable. However, be realistic. Consider your skills

> "When you do receive a job offer, just know it's not set in stone. If there are certain things that you don't like about your offer, you can negotiate."[22]
>
> —Kristen Winiarski, a writer who specializes in human resources and career advice

Open a Bank Account

If you don't yet have a bank account, opening one is a good idea once you start looking for work. Many businesses prefer to use direct deposit to electronically pay to an employee's bank account. Even if you receive your pay as a paper check, it might be easier to deposit the money in an account than to get a bank to cash the check. A bank account provides you a safe place for your money. Additionally, if you need cash you can take it out, or you can pay for items using a debit card, which takes the money from your account.

To open an account, you can go to a bank with your ID and some money for an initial deposit. If you are under eighteen, you will need a parent as a joint owner on the account. It is also possible to open a bank account online, but you will need to enter all of your information. When opening an account, compare the details of accounts at different banks. Decide which account is best for you based on answers to questions such as does the bank charge monthly fees on the account, are you required to keep a minimum balance, and what are the ATM fees? Once you've decided, open your account and get ready to see it grow with hard-earned money from your job.

and experience, how easily the employer could find others to fill the position, and how much you want to work there. A 2021 survey by the staffing firm ManpowerGroup is also worth noting. In that survey, 69 percent of employers said they were having difficulty finding the right employees for their business needs. In these conditions, prospective employees may have more leverage to negotiate for terms they consider to be more favorable, but there are no guarantees.

First, determine whether what you want is reasonable. Compare the salary and benefits of similar jobs at other companies. If what you want is not out of line, then decide what reason you will give when asked why the employer should meet your request. Having special skills or experience for the job might be one reason. Next, call your point of contact and begin the negotiation, clearly expressing that you want the job but would like to discuss a few changes. Yale University's Officer of Career Strategy recommends:

Use a friendly business tone, staying calm, and professional throughout the conversation. Express your enthusiasm for the position and reinforce your desire to be part of their team. Negotiate the base salary first, and save the most difficult issues for last. . . . If your terms are met, it is assumed that you will accept. It is unethical to negotiate if you have no intention of accepting the position.[23]

Negotiating can be nerve-wracking, but remember the worst that can happen is that the hiring manager says the employer cannot meet your requests. If this is the case, you must determine whether the job is still worth it to you. You can still accept the job, without the employer meeting your requests, if it is one you really want or need.

First Day

Once you've accepted a job, it is time to work. The first day of any job can be both exciting and a little scary, mostly because you don't know exactly what to expect. To help calm your nerves,

A new employee fills out paperwork. For most people, the first day on the job involves some type of administrative paperwork.

leave yourself plenty of time to get ready, and plan on arriving a few minutes early. Wear the correct clothing for the type of job. Remember to bring your identification, Social Security card, and bank account information. The employer will use this information for taxes and to set up a method of payment. Arrive with a positive attitude, ready to show interest in learning your job and meeting your new coworkers.

The first day on most jobs involves administrative paperwork and possibly starting some basic job training. In 2020 Amaya showed up to her first day at a Dunkin' Donuts restaurant. She was on time and wearing the right clothes—white polo shirt and jeans, as they had told her in the interview. She was nervous, because she did not know anyone who worked there and had not worked at Dunkin' Donuts before. Her job was to work at the drive-through and front register, taking and filling orders and providing customers with their food and drinks. The assistant manager gave her a brown visor and a name tag to wear, then had her fill out tax and payment paperwork. After that, she immediately began the job training. "The first thing they had me do was learn the registers. . . . They had me taking a few orders and they had me wearing the headset so I could hear everything going on. . . . To be a thousand percent honest, I was so overwhelmed . . . there were so many buttons,"[24] Amaya recalls. The rest of the day was a blur for her because there was so much to learn and do, but by the end of the day, she felt she was getting into a routine and was familiar with many duties. For the rest of her first week, she continued to learn all the aspects of the job. Additionally, she was required to watch training videos on how to make specific drinks, brew coffee, and brew iced tea. Within a week, she was comfortable in the job and continued working there for over two years.

No matter what the first-day experience is, remember that it is an accomplishment. Starting a new job after the journey to it is something to be proud of doing. Now it is time to make the most of the job—giving it your all, gaining experience, and making money.

CHAPTER SIX

Remote Work

Harrison Cain landed a job as a sales development representative in 2020 right after his graduation from college. The job interview and training were all done remotely. The job is also a remote-work position. He never expected to be working this way. But it has gone well. "As a sales team, we talk every day over zoom and with the wider team, virtual quizzes, Friday beers and group idea sessions have allowed us to build a great team environment,"[25] Cain says.

Cain is one of the increasing number of people who work remotely, meaning not in the company's offices and usually from home. Some jobs—for example, restaurant cooks and servers, factory and warehouse workers, car mechanics, dentists, and the like—cannot be done remotely. These jobs require in-person work or interaction. Remote jobs, however, can be done without in-person interaction. These are mostly office jobs that rely on computers, phones, and videoconferencing platforms.

The number of remote workers significantly increased during the COVID-19 pandemic shutdowns that began in 2020. During the pandemic, many businesses closed, but many others continued to operate with employees working from home. Studies by experts at the National Bureau of Economic Research estimate that remote work accounted for about 50 percent of paid work hours during April through December 2020, compared with 5 percent before the pandemic. By 2022, according to the career research company Zippia, about 22 percent of employees were still working remotely. Many employers and employees have continued this arrangement—or a hybrid of workplace and remote work—because it suits their needs. But some businesses—among them Google, Twitter, and Citigroup—are backing away from remote work and requiring employees to return to the office, either full time or part time.

From the Employee Perspective

Employee reaction has had much to do with the continuation of remote work. According to a 2022 survey by the remote work company FlexJobs, 44 percent of respondents said they know at least one person who has quit or is planning to quit a job because their company is requiring them to return to the office. This survey also found that 24 percent of workers would be willing to take a 10 to 20 percent pay cut in order to work from home, and 21 percent would forgo some vacation time to work at home. To retain employees, some companies continue to offer some form of remote work.

A young woman works in a designated workspace in her home. An increasing number of people work remotely, often from a home office.

The Etiquette of Online Meetings

Remote workers can expect to take part in a lot of online meetings. To get the most out of these meetings, it's worth following some basic rules of etiquette. Even though you're working from the comfort of home, you still need to be professional. Find a quiet space that will allow you to take part without constant interruptions. Also, make sure that whatever is visible behind you is work appropriate.

Dress also matters. Wear the clothes you would wear if you were in the office. There have been plenty of stories about remote workers wearing office attire on the top half of their bodies but not on the bottom half. Experts caution against doing this. If for any reason you have to stand up or move, you're going to wish you had dressed appropriately.

While in the meeting, keep the camera on so people can see you, and mute yourself when you're not talking to avoid unwanted background noise. When you are talking, be sure to look at the camera. Turn off notifications from messaging applications and phone ringtones. Always keep in mind that online meetings are professional meetings and should always be treated that way.

For employees, the positives of remote work are many. They do not need to drive or use any other transportation to get to work, saving time and money. They have more flexibility to schedule childcare, errands, and other activities around their workday. Remote work can be done from anywhere with a decent internet connection, which means people can work from another country, at a friend's house, or even while on vacation. A worker named Leo writes on his blog:

> Working remotely from home has changed how I live. Like most, I used to trek to work and back, wasting two to three hours daily, for years. I left around 7 am and came back around 6:30 pm. Most people follow this regime. At the start of the covid epidemic, I was lucky to switch to working remotely. As a software engineer, I can work from anywhere. . . . I get to have my espresso, take care of my 7 months old daughter, and eat a delicious breakfast, all before starting my workday.[26]

There are also some negatives connected with working at home. Not everyone lives in a house or apartment that is conducive to remote work. There might not be enough space or enough quiet for doing a full day's work. At home, many possible distractions can disrupt work, making it harder to focus than in an office setting.

Technology can also be a problem. Not everyone who works at home has a modern computer or good internet connection. Lastly, many remote workers say they miss in-person interactions with other employees. Kristen Painter, a deputy business editor at the *Star Tribune* in Minneapolis, writes of her time working remotely:

> I realized that I missed communicating face-to-face with the outside world, especially my colleagues. I happen to like them a lot, and our e-mail exchanges are a poor substitute. I wanted to know what they thought of a variety of global current events, or how their wedding planning was going, or if their elderly parents were healthy and well, but there's no good way to facilitate those sort of candid, casual conversations virtually.[27]

Another possible downside for remote workers is how not being in the office might affect their career objectives. Studies show that managers generally prefer to have employees working on-site. For instance, in a 2021 study by the Society for Human Resource Management, 72 percent of supervisors said they would prefer to have all of their employees working on-site. Additionally, 62 percent said they think full-time remote work harms their employees' career objectives by, for example, reducing the potential for promotion.

From the Employer Perspective

Employers have also spent time pondering the upsides and downsides of remote work as they try to assess its effects on their business. With fewer people in the office, some businesses have been able to save money by reducing or eliminating office space.

This in turn means less money spent on utilities, furniture, and various workplace amenities. Remote work also gives employers a larger pool of qualified people to choose from; people who do not live in the region can be considered for jobs. Employers say that remote work also translates to less wasted time. Online meetings, phone calls, texting, and emails tend to focus primarily on work rather than drift into office politics and gossip.

However, as with employees, employers do see negative aspects of remote work. Employers have less insight into work being done at home. They cannot know whether employees are using their time wisely and working a full day. It is also harder to establish team camaraderie when your employees are remote, since there is less interaction. As an example, Elon Musk, who became the CEO of Twitter in 2022, required that employees work forty hours a week on-site, unless he personally approved otherwise. His belief was that the highest quality of work could not be accomplished by working off-site.

Elon Musk is pictured speaking at the United States Air Force Academy in Colorado Springs, Colorado, in 2022. When Musk became CEO of Twitter in 2022, he required employees to work on-site unless he personally approved otherwise.

Maintaining Focus Working Remotely

Staying focused on work can be challenging when you work from home. Ashira Prossack, an internationally recognized communication trainer and coach, has several tips for staying focused. She suggests managing interruptions by turning off notifications on your phone and making sure that anyone who lives with you knows not to interrupt while you're working. She also suggests focusing on one task at a time. This will make it easier to complete each task.

Maintaining focus at home can be difficult. Prossack suggests taking regular breaks to help this process. She writes:

> The longer you work without a break, the harder it becomes to focus. Your brain needs time to disconnect from work periodically throughout the day. Be diligent about both scheduling and taking breaks, as simply putting them on your schedule and constantly working through them obviously does not have any benefit. When you find yourself needing to work through a scheduled break, be sure to still take that break once you've finished the task.

Ashira Prossack, "How to Stay Focused When Working from Home," *Forbes*, February 25, 2021. www.forbes.com.

For now, because of employee demand and changes implemented by companies in the past few years, some form of remote work is likely to remain at many organizations. Business owner Carrie Brinton believes remote work has become a permanent feature of the workplace. "Regardless of industry or business," Brinton says, "every employer must be prepared and ready to embrace a remote workforce model to some degree in order to remain competitive—or possibly even survive."[28]

Future of Remote Work

Even with more people returning to offices as restrictions have eased from the COVID-19 pandemic, most experts believe remote work will remain an integral part of the workplace. However, the trend seems to be an increase in hybrid work and a decrease in full-time remote work. This was the finding of a 2021 survey done by the global management consulting firm McKinsey & Company. McKinsey surveyed one hundred executives in various industries and countries and found that nine out of ten executives envision a hybrid model going forward.

Other research has had similar findings. The Stanford Institute for Economic Policy Research found that about 70 percent of firms, from small companies to multinationals like Apple, plan to implement forms of hybrid working arrangements. Nicholas Bloom, one of the study's authors, writes:

> "Hybrid arrangements balance the benefits of being in the office in person—greater ability to collaborate, innovate and build culture—with the benefits of quiet and the lack of commuting that come from working from home."[29]
>
> —Nicholas Bloom, Stanford Institute for Economic Policy Research senior fellow and professor in Stanford's Department of Economics

Hybrid arrangements balance the benefits of being in the office in person—greater ability to collaborate, innovate and build culture—with the benefits of quiet and the lack of commuting that come from working from home. Firms often suggest employees work two days a week at home, focusing on individual tasks or small meetings, and three days a week in the office, for larger meetings, training and social events.[29]

A company meeting is conducted that includes both remote and in-office employees. Many companies now have some type of hybrid working arrangement.

First Day of Remote Worker

Whether hired to work remotely or on-site, the first few days are usually taken up with meeting coworkers and supervisors and going through some sort of orientation. Remote workers will likely also spend their first few days setting up software and any other technology needed for their daily tasks and for meetings.

This was Bryan Caragay's experience. Caragay lives in Austin, Texas, and works as a programmer at a company in California's Silicon Valley. On his first day of work, in 2020, he was at his computer and ready for his first scheduled meeting at 9:00 a.m. It shortly became clear that he was two hours early; he had forgotten about the time difference. He spent much of the day on video calls getting help with downloading and setting up software on his computer. Another part of the day was devoted to setting up email and watching introductory videos about the company's computer security and safety protocols. He met many people during the online meetings and video calls. He learned about the company's expectations regarding his hours and work as a remote worker. "I basically work until I get my work done, make sure I'm going to the meetings. . . . I'm excited that it's on your own. . . . I do really well when it's up to me to do the work,"[30] Caragay says of his first day.

> "I basically work until I get my work done."[30]
>
> —Bryan Caragay, a remote software programmer

Whether your job search results in a remote, hybrid, or on-site job, you can be proud of the work you did to get that job. The process of job search is challenging. It takes time, energy, and perseverance. It can also help you better understand your abilities, interests, and life goals. Ideally, the job will be all that you hope it will be. But if it's not, you'll know what to do and how to do it next time.

SOURCE NOTES

Introduction: Changing Market

1. Quoted in Andrew Keshner, "Arguably, It Is the Best Time to Be a Teen in Search of Summer Work," MarketWatch, August 9, 2022. www.marketwatch.com.
2. Quoted in Alex Christian, "Why 'Digital Literacy' Is Now a Workplace Non-Negotiable," BBC, September 26, 2022. www.bbc.com.
3. James Sancto, "Adaptability: The Skill for Change," We Make Change, 2021. www.wemakechange.org.

Chapter One: What Kind of Job Do You Want?

4. Quoted in Dusty Baxter-Wright, "How I Got My First Job In: Race-horse Training," *Cosmopolitan*, June 15, 2018. www.cosmopolitan.com.
5. Peter Vogt, "Use Career Assessments Wisely—or Not at All," Monster, 2022. www.monster.com.
6. Quoted in Dusty Baxter-Wright, "How I Got My First Job In: Group Travel Tour Guiding," *Cosmopolitan*, May 25, 2018. www.cosmopolitan.com.
7. Quoted in Baxter-Wright, "How I Got My First Job In: Group Travel Tour Guiding."

Chapter Two: Preparation

8. Quoted in Kristi DePaul, "How to Get Your Resume Noticed (and Out of the Trash Bin)," *Ascend*, September 2020. https://hbr.org.
9. DePaul, "How to Get Your Resume Noticed (and Out of the Trash Bin)."
10. Ahmed Ishaque, "How I Got a Google Offer at 18," Medium, October 7, 2022. https://medium.com.

Chapter Three: Search and Apply

11. Quoted in Dusty Baxter-Wright, "How I Got My First Job In: Video Game Directing," *Cosmopolitan*, October 29, 2018. www.cosmopolitan.com.
12. Quoted in Quora, "Does LinkedIn Really Help Get a Job? If Yes, What Are the Best Ways?," 2022. www.quora.com.
13. Quoted in Jennifer Post, "Everything You Need to Know About Job Searching in the Digital Age," Business News Daily, October 20, 2022. www.businessnewsdaily.com.

Chapter Four: Time for an Interview

14. Quoted in Job-Applications.com, "Starbucks Interview Questions and Tips," 2022. www.job-applications.com.
15. Ishaque, "How I Got a Google Offer at 18."
16. Quoted in Mary Dowd, "How Important Is Attitude in a Job Interview?," Chron, January 25. 2022. https://work.chron.com.
17. Alyse Kalish, "12 Different Ways to Calm Your Interview Nerves (Because You've Got This)," The Muse, 2022. www.themuse.com.
18. Quoted in Kiely Kuligowski, "Things You Should Never Do During and After a Job Interview," Business Daily, August 5, 2022. www.businessnewsdaily .com.
19. Ben Laker et al., "4 Tips to Nail a Virtual Job Interview," *Harvard Business Review*, March 4, 2021. https://hbr.org.

Chapter Five: An Offer and a Job

20. Elsa Scola, "My First Week Working at Amazon," Towards Data Science, September 10, 2020. https://towardsdatascience.com.
21. Indeed, "Guide: Next Steps After You Got a Job Offer," August 5, 2022. www.indeed.com.
22. Kristen Winiarski, "10 Rules for Negotiating a Job Offer," Best Colleges, June 30, 2022. www.bestcolleges.com.
23. Yale University Office of Career Strategy, "Job Offers & Salary Negotiation," 2022. https://ocs.yale.edu.
24. Amaya, *My First Day Working at Dunkin Donuts*, YouTube, 2021. www .youtube.com/watch?v=jtgD4pyDkBM.

Chapter Six: Remote Work

25. Harrison Cain, "Starting My First Job, During a Pandemic: Harrison's Story," FaultFixers, March 2, 2021. www.faultfixers.com.
26. Leo, "23. Why I Love Working Remotely," *Leo's Oasis* (blog), May 4, 2022. https://leoaudibert.com.
27. Kristen Painter, "Working from Home to Avoid Coronavirus: I Admit, I Miss People," *Minneapolis (MN) Star Tribune*, March 13, 2020. www.startribune .com.
28. Carrie Brinton, "Pros and Cons of the Remote Workforce Model," Yarro, February 5, 2022. https://yarro.org.
29. Nicholas Bloom, "Hybrid Is the Future of Work," Stanford Institute for Economic Policy Research, June 2021. https://siepr.stanford.edu.
30. Bryan Caragay, *My First Day Working Remote in Austin, Texas*, YouTube, September 25, 2020. www.youtube.com/watch?v=PNI26htZ16M.

benefits: In addition to wages or salaries, employee compensation that can include health insurance, vacation days, sick leave, and more.

cover letter: A document, written by a job applicant stating an interest in the job and his or her credentials, that is submitted with a résumé.

direct deposit: A method of payment that electronically submits money into a bank account.

hybrid work: A flexible work model that blends remote and on-site work.

internship: A short-term work experience (either paid or unpaid) offered to students and sometimes others by companies and other organizations.

negotiation: After an initial job offer, a discussion between the employer and job candidate concerning salary and benefits.

networking: The process of interacting and developing relationships with other people to develop potential professional contacts.

reference: A person who agrees to attest to the character and abilities of a job applicant.

remote work: An arrangement that allows an employee to work from home or other locations outside of the company's offices.

résumé: A written account of a person's career, education, and skills, used when applying for jobs.

JOB SEARCH RESOURCES

Bureau of Labor Statistics

www.bls.gov

This government website gives information about all types of careers. It provides the projected growth rate of the careers, average pay, and other related information.

CareerOneStop

www.careeronestop.org

A US government–sponsored website that provides information about careers, a job search tool, and a "Young Adult" page specifically tailored to young adults who are searching for jobs.

JobHat

https://teens.jobhat.com

This website is a job search site with a section that specifically focuses on jobs for teenagers.

LinkedIn

www.linkedin.com

This is an online website for career and social networking. On the site, there are organizations to follow, individual professionals to link with, and the ability to search for jobs.

Monster

www.monster.com

On this career website, employers can post jobs, and users can view and apply for the jobs online.

My Perfect Cover Letter

www.myperfectcoverletter.com

This website provides free templates for building a cover letter. You are given prompts to input, such as name, job title, and experience, and it outputs a letter.

Novorésumé

www.novoresume.com

Novorésumé is a free résumé site that provides a résumé builder that will produce a résumé for you based on the information you input.

Resume Genius
www.resumegenius.com
Resume Genius provides free templates for creating résumés. Additionally, it includes samples that people can view to get an idea of what to include for work experiences, skills, and education.

Snagajob
www.snagajob.com
This is a job search website that is tailored to youth, with many entry-level jobs. You can use a filter to find jobs that are in the location and field you desire.

SportsCareerFinder
www.sportscareerfinder.com
SportsCareerFinder is a job search site that specifically includes sports and recreation job offerings. On this site, you can tailor the search to your parameters.

ZipRecruiter
www.ziprecruiter.com
ZipRecruiter is an employment marketplace for job seekers and employers. You can search and apply for jobs on this site.

FOR MORE INFORMATION

Books

Richard Bolles, *What Color Is Your Parachute? 2022: Your Guide to a Lifetime of Meaningful Work and Career Success*. Berkeley, CA: Ten Speed, 2021.

Vivian Foster, *Life Skills for Teens: The Ultimate Guide for Young Adults on How to Manage Money, Cook, Clean, Find a Job, Make Better Decisions, and Everything You Need to Be Independent*. Star Spark, 2022.

Fran Hauser, *Embrace the Work, Love Your Career: A Guided Workbook for Realizing Your Career Goals with Clarity, Intention, and Confidence*. Oakland, CA: Collective Book Studio, 2022.

Paul Tieger et al., *Do What You Are: Discover the Perfect Career for You Through the Secrets of Personality Type*. Boston, MA: Little, Brown Spark, 2021.

Internet Sources

Jamie Birt, "15 Best Jobs for a Teenager to Consider While in School," Indeed, October 24, 2022. www.indeed.com.

Future Learn, "How to Network to Improve Your Career," September 15, 2020. www.futurelearn.com.

Tom Garencer, "Teenage Resume Examples (Also with No Work Experience)," Zety, August 29, 2022. https://zety.com.

Post University, "7 Essential Tips to Get a Job After College," July 5, 2022. https://post.edu.

Youth.gov, "Career Exploration and Skill Development." https://youth.gov.

INDEX